CONSPIRACY!

by Charlie Samuels

Crabtree Publishing Company

www.crabtreebooks.com

Crabtree Publishing Company

www.crabtreebooks.com

Author: Charlie Samuels
Project Coordinator: Kathy Middleton
Editors: Adrianna Morganelli, Tim Cooke
Proofreader: Crystal Sikkens
Designer: Lynne Lennon
Cover Design: Margaret Amy Salter
Picture Researcher: Andrew Webb
Picture Manager: Sophie Mortimer
Art Director: Jeni Child
Editorial Director: Lindsey Lowe
Children's Publisher: Anne O'Daly
**Production Coordinator and
    Prepress Technician:** Samara Parent
Print Coordinator: Katherine Berti

Photographs
Cover: Dreamstime: Zrfphoto (alien);
    Shutterstock (background and agent)
Interior: Alamy: Jason O. Watson 20; **Corbis:**
Bettmann 22; **Getty Images:** Hulton Arhive 24; **Library
of Congress:** 14, 15; **NASA:** GRIN 26, 27; **Public
Domain:** 4, 17, 29, Paul Mellon Collection in the Yale
Center for British Art/Google Art Project: 6, 7; **Robert
Hunt Library:** 10, 11, 18, 19, 25; **Shutterstock:** Dan
Howell 28; **Thinkstock:** Hemera 16–17, Photodisc 23,
Photos.com 8, 9; **Topfoto:** Fortean 21, Museum of
London 13, Topham Picturepoint 12, World History
Archive 5.

Library and Archives Canada Cataloguing in Publication

Samuels, Charlie, 1961-
    Conspiracy! / Charlie Samuels.

(Mystery files)
Includes index.
Issued also in electronic formats.
ISBN 978-0-7787-1126-1 (bound).--ISBN 978-0-7787-1130-8 (pbk.)

    1. History--Miscellanea--Juvenile literature. 2. Conspiracies--
Juvenile literature. I. Title. II. Series: Mystery files (St. Catharines,
Ont.)

D21.3.S36 2013   j902   C2012-908507-3

Library of Congress Cataloging-in-Publication Data

Samuels, Charlie, 1961-
  Conspiracy! / Charlie Samuels.
      pages cm. -- (Mystery files)
  Includes index.
  ISBN 978-0-7787-1126-1 (reinforced library binding : alk. paper)
-- ISBN 978-0-7787-1130-8 (pbk. : alk. paper) -- ISBN
978-1-4271-9278-3 (electronic pdf : alk. paper) -- ISBN
978-1-4271-9202-8 (electronic html : alk. paper)
  1. Conspiracy theories--Juvenile literature 2. Conspiracies--
Juvenile literature. I. Title.

HV6275.S26 2013
001.9--dc23

2012049704

Crabtree Publishing Company
www.crabtreebooks.com   1-800-387-7650

Published in Canada
Crabtree Publishing
616 Welland Ave.
St. Catharines, ON
L2M 5V6

Published in the United States
Crabtree Publishing
PMB 59051
350 Fifth Avenue, 59th Floor
New York, New York 10118

Published by CRABTREE PUBLISHING COMPANY in 2013
Copyright © 2013 Brown Bear Books Ltd

Printed in Canada/012013/MA20121217

Contents

Introduction

On September 11, 2001, Muslim **terrorists** crashed airplanes in New York City, Washington, D.C., and Pennsylvania. Or did they? While most people believe this version of events, a few claim that the U.S. government was behind the attacks. Some believe that the United States wanted to justify military operations overseas. These people claim to find holes in the official explanation of the events.

Who was really responsible for the destruction on 9/11?

A reluctance to believe the official version of events is not unique. There are people who question even things that everyone else believes to be true. They believe the public are victims of **conspiracies** by governments and officials who do not want people to know the truth about particular events.

Common Theories

This book examines some of the most common conspiracy **theories**. You'll meet the man who may really have written the plays of William Shakespeare. You'll learn about a secret society that may govern the world. You'll discover doubts about who killed not one but two U.S. presidents.

Far more people do not believe conspiracy theories than do believe them. But is there any room for doubt? After reading this book, you'll be able to make up your own mind.

Titus Oates tried to stir up hatred toward British Catholics.

The Great Fire of LONDON

The summer of 1666 in London, England, was hot and dry. But when a fire broke out at the king's baker's home in Pudding Lane on September 2, many suspected it was not an accident. London was full of rumors of plots and attacks.

Crowded boats carry Londoners across the Thames to safety.

The Great Fire of London, as it became known, burned for three days. Fanned by strong winds, it burned the dry timber buildings of the old city. The fire destroyed more than 13,500 buildings, including the offices of the city authorities.

England's Enemies

As the fire burned, the rumors began. The baker claimed his ovens were out and could not have started the fire. Many people blamed Catholics. English Catholics had opposed the **restoration** of the Protestant King Charles II to the throne in 1660. Others thought the fire was the work of foreigners. The French supported Catholic claims to the throne. The Dutch were at war with the English over trading rights. Some people claimed that the fire was started to prepare the way for an invasion by enemy troops—but no invasion ever came.

Mystery File:

FORGED DOCUMENT

More than 150 years after the fire, a **manuscript** was found that claimed Catholics had plotted to kill King Charles II. In reality, a Protestant plotter named Titus Oates had faked the document to try to stir up hatred toward Catholics.

Mystery words...

restoration: the return of something to its previous condition

Who was SHAKESPEARE?

William Shakespeare is the most famous playwright in the world. The plays he wrote in the 16th and 17th centuries are still performed. But were they really written by a little-known country boy?

Shakespeare was a real man, but did he write the plays?

The argument has raged for centuries. Famous writers such as Mark Twain and Charles Dickens are among those who wondered if Shakespeare could have produced so many masterpieces. We know that Shakespeare was an actor, and that he came from the small town of Stratford-upon-Avon, in England. He does not seem to have been well educated, but his plays reveal a great knowledge of history. Where did Shakespeare learn such information?

Mystery words...

contemporaries: people who all live at the same time

Also, the plays are refined and witty. Some people say only a gentleman would have those qualities, not a simple actor.

Lack of Evidence

The doubts have been encouraged because there is no evidence to prove the actor Shakespeare was the same person that wrote the plays. Some of the most famous plays,

Mystery File:
POSSIBLE AUTHOR

Francis Bacon (1561–1626) was a well educated politician and scientist. It was first suggested in the mid-19th century that Bacon wrote at least some of Shakespeare's plays. The idea stuck and is still around today.

like *Macbeth* and *Julius Caesar*, were published after Shakespeare's death. Others exist in slightly different versions. That has only added to the mystery.

Some people suggest that other **contemporaries** wrote the plays. The most common candidates are Christopher Marlowe, himself a famous playwright, and the scholar Francis Bacon.

Theater was the favorite form of entertainment during Shakespeare's time.

Burning the
REICHSTAG

Lubbe (standing) went on trial.

Adolf Hitler became chancellor of Germany in 1932, but he had no majority. In 1933, a fire in the German parliament allowed him to seize far greater powers.

The fire that broke out on February 27, 1933, destroyed the Reichstag. Hitler immediately blamed the fire on his political rivals, the communists. A Dutch communist, Marinus van der Lubbe, was

Mystery words...

dictator: a ruler with no limits to his or her power

found guilty of starting the fire, and was executed. In elections held a few days after the fire, Hitler's Nazi Party gained increased support. Hitler passed laws that gave him power as a virtual **dictator**. In reality, there was little evidence to connect the communists with the fire. Van der Lubbe was too simple-minded to have planned anything himself.

Nazi Germany was full of plots, many of which targeted Hitler. On July 20, 1944, Colonel Claus von Stauffenberg detonated a bomb at a meeting in an attempt to kill Hitler. It failed, because Hitler was shielded from the blast by a heavy table.

The True Story

The truth about the Reichstag fire only emerged in 2001. The Nazis had set fire to the Reichstag themselves and fixed the trial that followed. They had burned down the parliament so they had an excuse to attack their opponents. Some 25,000 of the Nazis' enemies were arrested after the fire. And Hitler's political power from then onward was secure.

The ruins of the Reichstag smolder after the fire.

Jack the RIPPER

For four months in 1888, the streets of Victorian **London** were stalked by a serial killer. Nicknamed "Jack the Ripper," he murdered at least five women by slitting their throats, then cut up their bodies. Why does this unknown murderer still grab the public's attention?

More than 120 years after Jack the Ripper stalked London's East End, his identity remains a mystery. His nickname came from a letter to the police that claimed to be from the killer. The letter was signed "Jack." It was never proved to be **authentic**. London's Metropolitan Police named four main suspects, but that has not stopped others from **speculating** on the true identity of the killer.

Mystery words...

speculating: making decisions without clear evidence

Many Suspects

One suggestion is that the murderer was a butcher or surgeon, because of the way the victims' bodies were cut up. Among the many suspects named by people who have studied the case is a British prince: Albert Victor, the grandson of Queen Victoria. Other possibilities are the artist Walter Sickert and the author Lewis Carroll. Was the killer a prominent citizen whose identity has been hushed up? We may never know. The identity of "Jack" remains a mystery.

Did a **cover-up** protect the identity of the killer? We don't know! The **list of suspects keeps growing**. One recent suggestion is that the killer was Charles Cross, a cartman who found the body of the **first victim**, Polly Nichols.

The murders took place in the streets of London's East End.

Death of LINCOLN

On April 14, 1865, President Abraham Lincoln went to the theater. During the U.S. Civil War, Lincoln guided the northern states, known as the Union, to victory. John Wilkes Booth, who supported the defeated South, shot and fatally wounded the president.

Booth was an actor. He was well known for his sympathies with the South, known as the Confederacy. The Southern states had broken away from the Union because they did not want to abolish slavery. But they had no choice when the Union won the war and Lincoln passed the

Lincoln lies on his deathbed.

law which freed the slaves. Booth and others who shared his support for the South plotted to kill Lincoln and his vice president, William Seward. After shooting Lincoln, Booth was hunted down and shot by police. The other plotters were rounded up, tried, and executed. But even at the time, many Americans suspected that the plot was planned by a higher political power.

John Wilkes Booth was an eager supporter of the Confederacy.

Mystery File:
MANY SUSPECTS

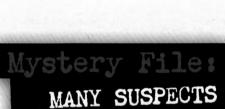

Suggested suspects on the Union side that may have wanted Lincoln out of the way were the popular commander Ulysses S. Grant, Wall Street financiers, the Catholic Church, and even Lincoln's secretary of state Edwin Stanton.

Who Did It?

Many people wanted Lincoln dead. Southern leaders, such as former Confederate president Jefferson Davis, were high on the list of suspects. Had the Confederacy planned the **assassination**? In the North, suggested plotters included secret organizations and individuals who stood to benefit from Lincoln's death.

Mystery words...

assassination: a murder inspired by the victim's position

A Secret SOCIETY

During the 18th century, secret societies were a rage in Europe and America. Most were harmless. But one is still suspected of having secret influence over the world's government and economics.

The German poet Goethe may have belonged to the secret society.

The Illuminati ("Enlightened Ones") were founded by a German law professor on May 1, 1776. Dr. Adam Weishaupt wanted the organization to spread new ideas about a society based on **reason**. These ideas were part of a movement known as the Enlightenment. The Enlightenment challenged many ideas of the powerful Catholic Church that controlled much of Europe at the time. The Illuminati argued that Catholic beliefs were based on superstition, not reason.

Mystery words...

reason: a way of thinking based on logic and facts

The Illuminati Spread

The Illuminati grew quickly. It aimed to place its members in positions of political and social importance, where they could influence change. In the United States, the Illuminati provoked protests from those who thought they threatened the new United States. It is still not known for sure who was or was not a member of the Illuminati. Some people still suspect that many of the world's most powerful individuals belong to the organization, and say we should all be suspicious of their aims.

A modern version of the Illuminati is the Bilderberg Group, formed in 1954. Each year some of the world's important people are invited to its meeting. The discussions are secret, so some people wonder what the group is plotting.

The Bilderberg Group took its name from the hotel where it first met.

Attack on
PEARL HARBOR

The Japanese attack on Pearl Harbor in December 1941 brought the United States into World War II. U.S. President Roosevelt wanted to join the war. Did he allow the attack to happen so he could get his way?

President Roosevelt signs the declaration of war.

The Japanese attack on the U.S. naval base in Hawaii was as devastating as it was unexpected. Within 24 hours, President Franklin D. Roosevelt announced that the United States was at war with Japan, and with its German and Italian allies. But some military leaders and Roosevelt's enemies suspected that he had deliberately ignored **intelligence** reports of a likely Japanese attack.

Mystery words...

intelligence: information learned from enemy communications

Plot or Accident?

It was true that tensions with the Japanese had been building for some time. There were even rumors of an attack on a U.S. base. Pearl Harbor received no warnings. But secret intelligence intercepted by U.S. forces led them to believe that any attack would come in the Philippines. In addition, problems with radio transmitters at Pearl Harbor prevented final warnings from getting through. There is no evidence, however, that the president had anything to do with such a delay.

Another rumor about the Japanese attack was that the British learned about it but did not warn the Americans. It is said the British wanted the United States to be forced into the war. U.S. support was a great boost for the allies.

A warship burns after the Japanese attack.

Aliens at
ROSWELL

Roswell, New Mexico, is a remote desert town, but it is near to many military installations. Did law enforcement services there really discover evidence of alien visits to Earth in July 1947?

A violent thunderstorm hit Roswell in the summer of 1947. Local rancher "Mac" Brazel found small bits of strange material scattered over his land. It resembled lightweight aluminum, but it could not be burned or cut.

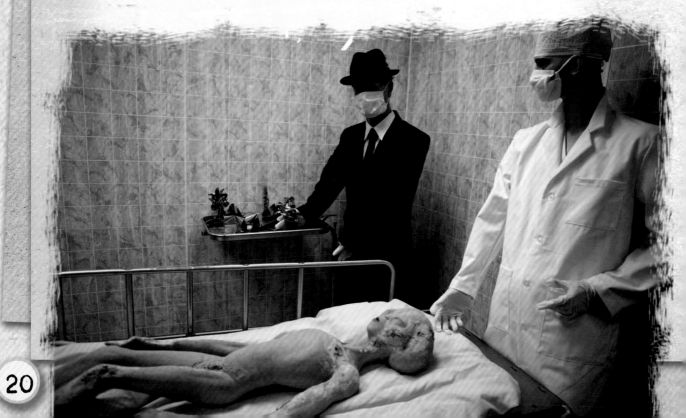

The Roswell newspaper reports the discovery in July 1947.

A Flying Saucer

When neighboring land was examined, searchers claimed to find a spaceship with four dying or dead aliens close by. Witnesses said the aliens were under five feet (1.5 meters) tall, and had slits for eyes. The army at a nearby base announced that a "flying disk" had been found. But soon that story changed. Now the army claimed that the wreckage came from a high-altitude radar balloon. But what about the aliens? Many people believe they have never been explained.

Mystery File: AREA 51

Area 51 is a classified U.S. military base in Nevada, near Las Vegas. The latest aircraft and weapons are tested there. But the secret base has become a tourist destination. It was made famous by the movie *Independence Day* (1996).

Mystery words...

alien: a being from another planet

21

Howard Hughes'
BILLIONS

Howard Hughes (1905-1976) inherited a fortune and made even more money in the movie and aviation industries. As he grew older, his behavior became increasingly odd. After his death, the mysteries surrounding Hughes grew.

Hughes' business dealings made him hugely rich.

ughes was one of the richest people in the world. He was a movie producer and owned an airline. But by the 1930s, Hughes was becoming mentally ill. He moved into a hotel in Las Vegas, and rarely left it. He became obsessed with bugs and hygiene. He lived closed off from society. Only his assistants saw him. Many were **Mormons**; they were referred to as the "Mormon **Mafia**." There were rumors that Hughes was also involved with the leaders of organized crime.

The Mormon church is based in Salt Lake City.

Lasting Mystery

Everything about Hughes was a mystery. Even his memoirs, which appeared in 1972, were a hoax. When he died, a mysterious handwritten will turned up. It left money to the Mormon Church and to a gas station owner named Melvin Dummar. But a court said that the will was a forgery. Hughes' money went to his 22 cousins.

Mystery words...

Mafia: a secret group that runs organized crime

Assassination in
DALLAS

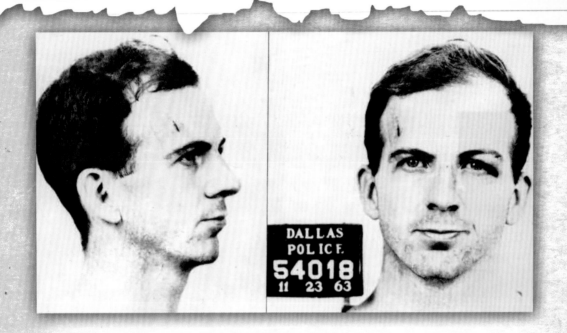

U.S. President John F. Kennedy was shot dead in Dallas, Texas, on November 22, 1963. A culprit was soon arrested. But even today many people still think there was a conspiracy behind the shooting that remains unsolved.

Two bullets hit Kennedy as he drove in an open car. He died instantly. That's about all anyone agrees on. A former soldier named Lee Harvey Oswald was arrested nearby. But before he went on trial, Oswald himself was

Mystery words...

culprit: a person who commits a crime

shot dead. Soon rumors suggested that Oswald had not operated alone. They say one gunman could not have fired the shots so accurately and so quickly.

Powerful Enemies

Kennedy was having political difficulties with the Soviet bloc and Cuba. Perhaps these communist powers were behind the hit. Kennedy's attempt to stop organized crime may also have made him enemies among the Mafia.

Mystery File:
FBI ENEMIES

The director of the Federal Bureau of Investigation (FBI) was J. Edgar Hoover. Hoover hated President Kennedy. A report criticized the FBI for not investigating the shooting fully. Some people say the FBI was even involved in the plot.

Kennedy and his wife Jackie begin the fatal parade.

The Moon Landing
HOAX

On July 20, 1969, half a billion people watched grainy TV images as Neil Armstrong became the first human to set foot on the Moon. It is one of the most famous events of modern history—but some people say it never happened.

The doubters claim the National Aeronautical and Space Administration (NASA) faked the Moon landing in a movie studio. They claim there are clues in photos of the Apollo 11 mission. Perhaps NASA wanted to get more funding from the U.S. government. Or perhaps the government wanted to claim victory in its race with the Soviet Union to conquer space.

Astronaut Buzz Aldrin was the second human to set foot on the Moon.

Evidence of a Hoax?

People say there are no stars above
the Moon in images of the mission.
They claim the dark sky must be a
backdrop. But in fact the **lunar module**
landed on the dayside of the Moon,
where it was too bright to see stars.
Why does the U.S. flag appear to move
in zero gravity? That's because driving
the flagpole into the hard lunar surface
left it vibrating for a while.

Mystery File:
POSITIVE PROOF

Apollo 11 and
five more missions left
hardware on the Moon. That
hardware can still be seen
from spacecraft. And Apollo 11
brought back rocks older than
any on Earth. Aren't those
facts proof that the Moon
landing really did
take place?

Mystery words...

lunar module: a spacecraft built to land on the Moon's surface

The 9/11 Terrorist ATTACKS

The towers of the World Trade Center burn before collapsing.

On September 11, 2001, terrorists hijacked four aircraft. Two planes crashed into New York's World Trade Center, a third into the Pentagon in Washington, D.C. The fourth crashed in a field in Pennsylvania.

The worst terrorist attack on U.S. soil killed almost 3,000 people. The **Islamist** group al-Qaeda was blamed, but conspiracy theories started at once. A few people blamed the U.S. government saying it wanted more control over their lives. They said the towers of the World Trade Center fell so quickly after

Mystery words...

Islamist: an orthodox Muslim that believes society should be based on Islamic laws

the impact that they must have been brought down by explosives planted inside the buildings. They say the destruction at the Pentagon did not fit the shape of a large aircraft.

In fact, structural engineering explains why the towers fell. The impact of the planes started fires, and very high temperatures weakened the towers' steel supports, so the buildings collapsed. At the Pentagon, a **black box recorder** was recovered. It showed the airplane had indeed flown into the building.

The extensive damage to the west face of the Pentagon can be seen in this aerial photograph.

Glossary

alien A being from another planet

assassination A murder inspired by the victim's position

authentic Genuine or real

black box recorder A device carried on airplanes that records information about a flight

Civil War A war between the northern and southern U.S. states over the issue of slavery

conspiracies Secret plans to do something unlawful

contemporaries People who all live at the same time

cover-up A deliberate campaign to stop evidence from becoming known

culprit A person who commits a crime

dictator A ruler with no limits to his or her power

intelligence Information learned secretly from enemy communications

Islamist An orthodox Muslim that believes society should be based on Islamic laws

lunar module A spacecraft built to land on the Moon's surface

Mafia A secret group that runs organized crime

manuscript A hand-written document

military installation A facility servicing military forces, such as a base or training center

Mormon A member of the Church of Jesus Christ of Latter-day Saints

reason A way of thinking based on logic and facts

restoration The return of something to its previous condition

speculating Making decisions without clear evidence

terrorist Someone who uses violence to achieve a specific goal

theories Ideas that are used to explain something, like an event

Find Out More

BOOKS

Anderson, Jennifer Joline. *Jack the Ripper* (Unsolved Mysteries). Essential Library, 2012.

Fradin, Dennis B. *September 11, 2001* (Turning Points in U.S. history). Benchmark Books, 2009.

Robson, David. *The Kennedy Assassination* (Mysterious and Unknown). Referencepoint Press, 2008.

Southwell, David, and Sean Twist. *Unsolved Political Mysteries* (Mysteries and Conspiracies). Rosen Central, 2007.

Southwell, David, and Sean Twist. *Secret Societies* (Mysteries and Conspiracies). Rosen Central, 2007.

WEBSITES

30 Greatest Conspiracy Theories
A list from the British newspaper *The Daily Telegraph*
www.telegraph.co.uk/news/newstopics/howaboutthat/3483477/The-30-greatest-conspiracy-theories-part-1.html

Conspiracy Theories Top 10
Listverse.com guide to 10 international conspiracies
http://listverse.com/2007/08/21/top-10-conspiracy-theories/

The Appeal of Conspiracies
Scientific American article entitled "Why People Believe in Conspiracy Theories"
www.scientificamerican.com/article.cfm?id=why-people-believe-conspiracy-theories

Index